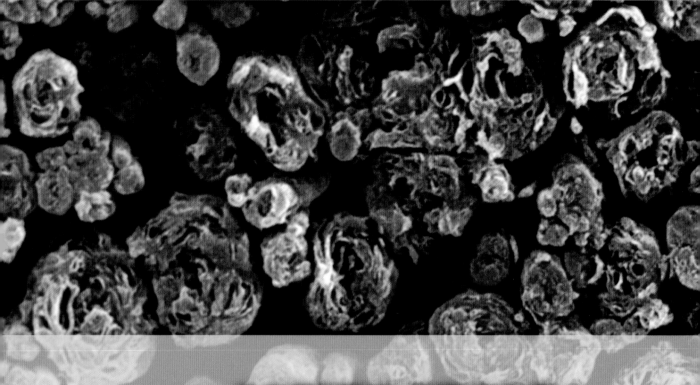

NERVOUS SYSTEM

GEORGE CAPACCIO

mc Marshall Cavendish
Benchmark

Marshall Cavendish Benchmark
99 White Plains Road
Tarrytown, New York 10591
www.marshallcavendish.us

Editor: Karen Ang
Publisher: Michelle Bisson
Art Director: Anahid Hamparian
Series Design by: Kay Petronio
Series Designer: Elynn Cohen

Library of Congress Cataloging-in-Publication Data
Capaccio, George.
The nervous system / by George Capaccio
p. cm. -- (The amazing human body)
Includes bibliographical references and index.
Summary: "Discusses the parts that make up the human nervous system, what can go wrong, how to treat those illnesses and diseases, and how to stay healthy"--Provided by publisher.
ISBN 978-0-7614-4039-0
1. Nervous system--Juvenile literature. 2. Nervous system--Diseases--Juvenile literature. I. Title.

QP361.5.K56 2010   612.8--dc22   2008037255

 = nerve cells from the brain stem

Front cover: The brain and the spinal cord   Back Cover: Nerve cells
Photo research by Tracey Engel
Front cover photo: Derek Berwin / Getty

The photographs in this book are used by permission and through the courtesy of: Getty Images: Dr. Fred Hossler, 1; 3D4Medical.com, 4, 7, 17, 38; Dennis Kunkel Microscopy, Inc., 6; 3D Clinic, 9, 18, 58; CMSP, 23, back cover; De Agostini, 10, 14, 19; Dr. David M. Phillips, 12; Scientifica, 13; artpartner-images, 16; Carol and Mike Werner/Visuals Unlimited, Inc., 20; Barbara Singer, 22; Nucleus Medical Art, Inc., 24, 27, 29, 35, 36, 40, 55, 59, 65; James Worrell, 26; Dr. John D. Cunningham/Visuals Unlimited, Inc., 43; Jeff Sherman, 45; Nick Veasey, 51; George Musil, 60; Barros & Barros, 62; Karen Knauer, 64; Patryce Bak, 67; Zia Soleil, 69; Philip Lee Harvey, 70; Jamie Grill, 71; B Busco, 72. Alamy: Scott Camazine, 46; Nucleus Medical Art, Inc., 50, 53; Jupiter Images/Comstock Images, 54; Collection CNRI / PHOTOTAKE, 56. Photo Researchers, Inc.: BSIP, 31, 41. James Cavallini, 32; Gary Carlson, 48. SuperStock: Image Source, 28.

Printed in Malaysia
123456

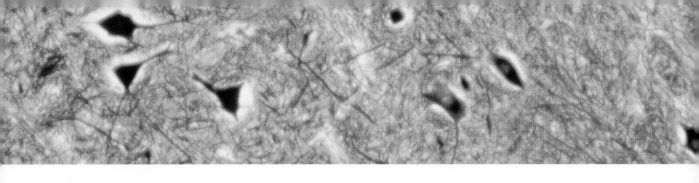

CONTENTS

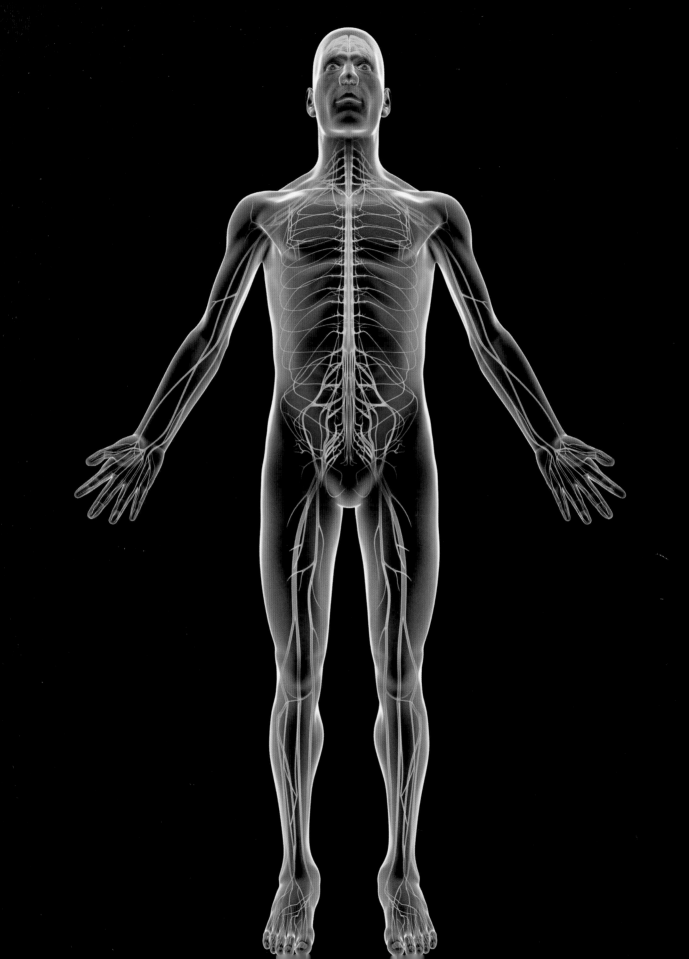

1

What Is the Nervous System?

The nervous system is responsible for all the processes that make human life possible. It lets us think, dream, and have a lifetime of memories. It also handles our most basic, involuntary actions and reactions like blinking our eyes, keeping our body at the right temperature, breathing, and making our heart beat. It is the body's way of communicating with itself and the outside world.

The human nervous system can be divided into two separate systems—the central nervous system (CNS) and the peripheral nervous system (PNS). The central nervous system includes the brain and the spinal cord. The peripheral nervous system is everything else. This

◄ *The human nervous system is made up of the brain, the spinal cord, and the networks of nerves running throughout the body.*

"everything else" includes all the nerves that connect the central nervous system with the muscles, glands, and organs of our bodies.

THE BRAIN

An adult brain weighs about 3 pounds (1.4 kilograms). It is roughly the size of a large grapefruit and kind of looks like a cauliflower. The human brain is probably the most complex organ in the body.

It has about 100 billion nerve cells, or neurons, and trillions of support cells called glia. If you could remove all 100 billion nerve cells and arrange them in a straight line, they would stretch for a distance of about 600 miles (1,000 kilometers). Of course, you would not be able to see this line since nerve cells are only visible under a microscope. Many scientists think that if you tried to count all of the neurons in the human brain, it would take you more than three thousand years.

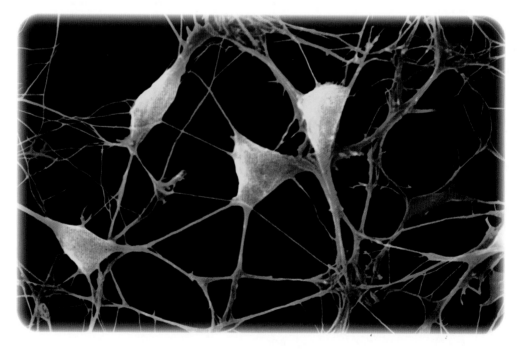

The activities of the billions of nerve cells in the brain are responsible for many of the important processes in the body.

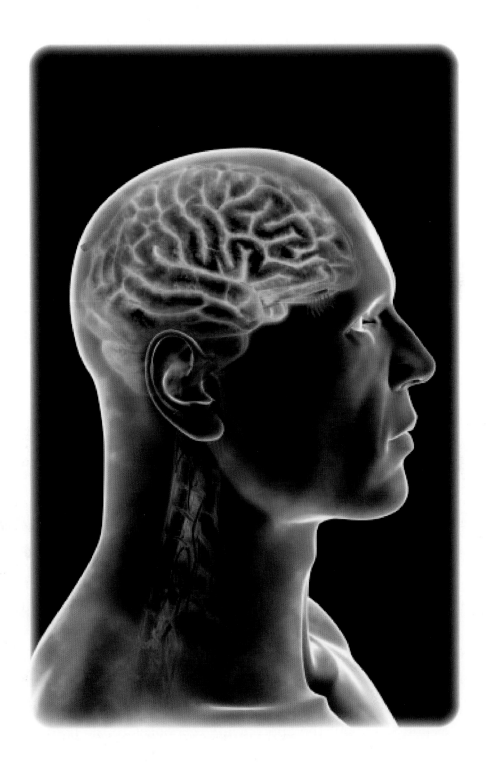

THE SPINAL CORD

The spinal cord is a long, bundle of nerves that carries nerve impulses back and forth between the brain and the rest of the body. It is about 17 inches (43 centimeters) long in women and 18 inches (45 cm) in men. It is about .5 inch (1.3 cm) wide.

The top of the spinal cord connects with the base of the brain at the brain stem. The lower end of the spinal cord is about two-thirds of the way down the spinal column. The spinal cord is safely contained within the spinal column, which is also called the spine or the vertebral column. The spine is made up of thirty-three bones called vertebrae. Each vertebra is separated from the one above and the one below by a disc of flexible, shock-absorbent tissue called cartilage. The spinal column is an important part of the body's skeletal system. It supports the skull and connects with the hips.

The spinal cord has thirty-one pairs of spinal nerves. With the exception of the top pair of nerves, the spinal nerves exit the spinal column through the spaces between the vertebrae. Spinal nerves conduct information to and from the spinal cord to the rest of the body.

THE PERIPHERAL NERVOUS SYSTEM

The peripheral nervous system is made up of all the nerves outside the central nervous system. These include the nerves that leave the brain and the spinal cord and extend to all parts of the body. Part of the job of the peripheral nervous system is to gather information from sensory receptors and relay, or send out, this information to the central nervous system. The messages are transmitted in the form of electrical signals, or nerve impulses.The central nervous system then interprets the messages it receives and sends out the appropriate responses to the body's glands, muscles, and organs.

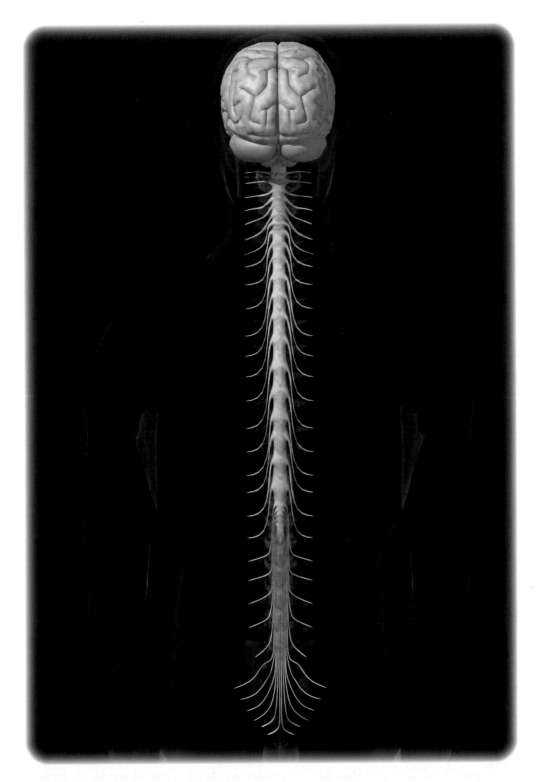

The spinal cord starts at the base of the brain and stretches down to the bottom of the spine.

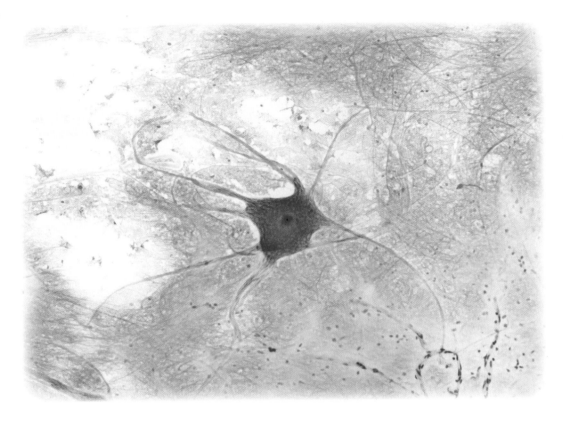

All neurons, or nerve cells, have a main cell body and long extensions called axons and dendrites.

neurons, all nerve cells have certain characteristics in common. They have a central part called a nucleus. The parts that extend from the nucleus are the axons and dendrites. Axons carry information—in the form of an electrical signal—away from the neuron to another neuron. Dendrites receive electrical signals from other neurons.

A typical neuron is about 10 microns wide, which is smaller than a period at the end of a sentence or the dot on top of a small letter "i." Though they are not very wide, neurons are the longest cells in the human body. The axon a neuron in the spinal cord that connects to a foot muscle can be about 3 feet (1 meter) long. Nerves are thin threads of neurons. These nerves create a kind of electrical circuitry in the body. Without it, we could not feel or respond to changes inside our body and in the world outside.

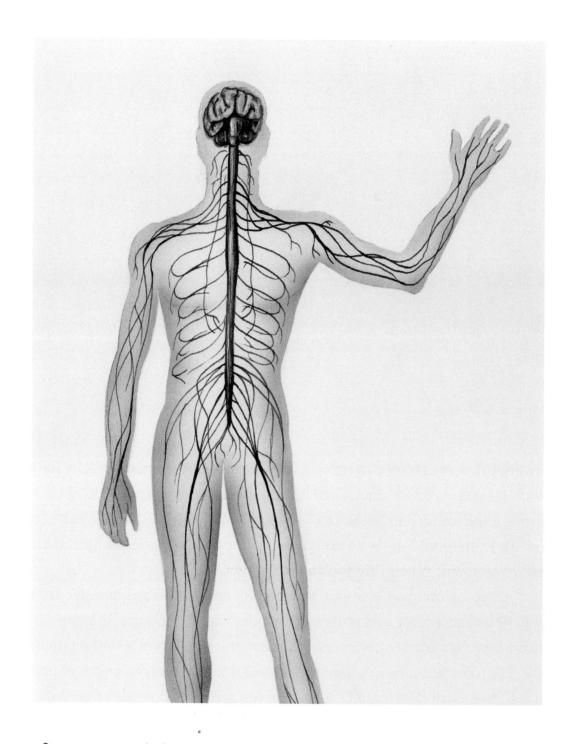

Some nerves control voluntary actions, such as moving the arm, while others assist the body in involuntary actions that support life.

There are different types of neurons. One way to classify neurons is by the number of extensions they have. Another way is by the direction in which the neurons send information. Motor, or efferent, neurons send information away from the central nervous system toward muscles and glands. Sensory, or afferent, neurons send information from sensory receptors toward the central nervous system. Interneurons send information between sensory and motor neurons and are mostly located in the brain and spinal cord.

Sensory neurons respond to stimuli from the environment and transmit an electrical signal to the spinal cord or the brain where the signal is interpreted. The brain then sends out an appropriate response through a pathway of motor neurons to a muscle or gland. This results in some kind of action or response. For example, we pull our hand away from something hot, or we smile with delight from the taste or smell of a favorite food.

NERVE IMPULSES

Suppose you get up in the middle of the night to get a drink of water. On the way to the kitchen, you stub your big toe on a table leg. Right away, sensory neurons in your big toe go into action.

Have you ever seen baseball fans do a "wave" during a game? That is when one section after another stands up and then sits down. This creates a wavelike motion that travels around the entire stadium. Or maybe you have stacked up a line of dominos and then knocked over the first one. What happens next? All the dominos fall, one by one.

The act of stubbing your toe has set off an electrical charge or pulse. Like the baseball stadium wave or the falling dominos, the pulse travels all the way down the axon of one neuron to the dendrites of the next

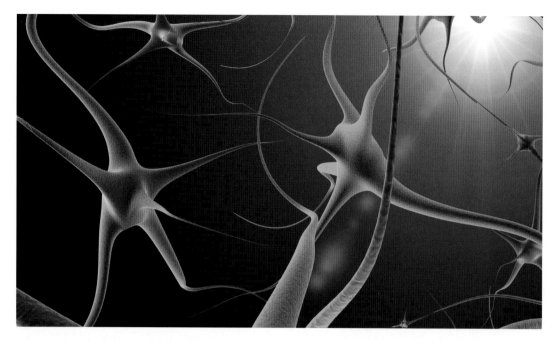

Nerve cells are always found alongside other nerve cells so that they can pass along signals and messages.

neuron in line, and so on until it reaches your spinal cord. From there, this nerve impulse travels up to your brain where the signal is received and interpreted. In a flash, your brain recognizes the sensation and you yell, "Ouch!" Of course, a similar process takes place if the original stimulus is something pleasurable like taking a hot shower on a cold morning. Then your response will be more like "Ahhh!"

Information in the form of electrical pulses travels at different speeds depending upon what types of neurons are activated. The speed of transmission can range from about 1.5 feet (0.5 m) per second to 394 feet (120 m) per second. The faster speed is equivalent to driving 268 miles (431 kilometers) per hour.

CROSSING THE GAP

At the end of every axon there is a tiny gap or space called a synapse. Synapses occur between neurons. (They also occur between a neuron and a muscle or gland.) When a nerve impulse reaches the end of an axon, it

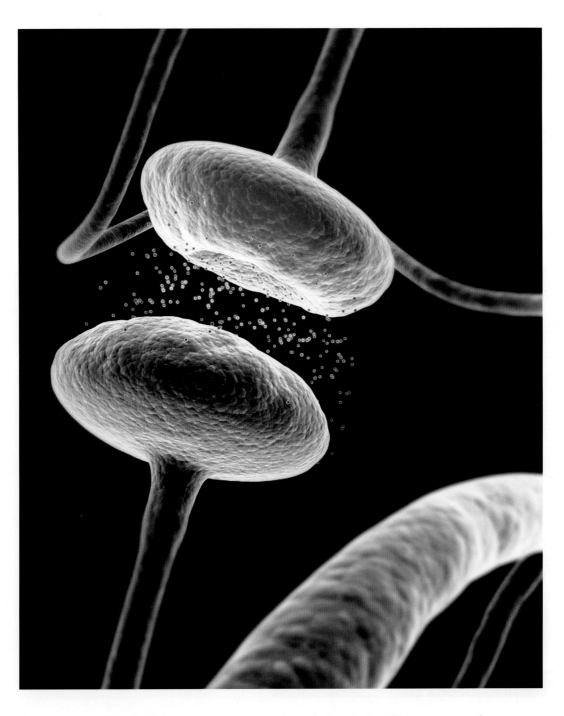

Messages are transmitted from neuron to neuron through chemicals called neurotransmitters that cross the synaptic gap between the neurons.

has to cross the synapse in order to continue on its way and to get picked up by the dendrites of the next neuron in line. So how does it do this? Imagine yourself trying to cross from one side of a river to the other side. You could try swimming. But a better choice would be to take a boat or use a bridge if there is one available.

Nerve impulses cannot do any of these things to cross a synapse. They have to rely on special chemicals called neurotransmitters. These chemical messengers are stored in the body of the nerve cell. When an action potential, or nerve impulse, reaches the end of an axon, the cell releases these chemicals. Molecules of neurotransmitters travel across

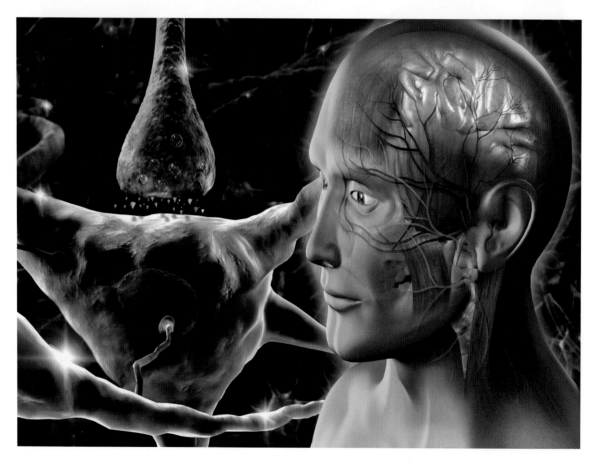

Chemical and electrical signals are constantly moving through the body and transmitting messages to the brain.

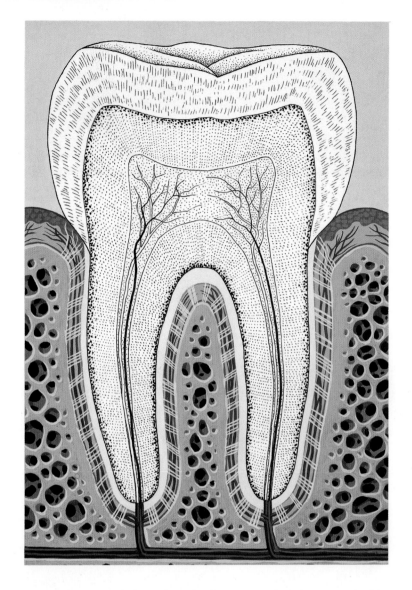

Teeth have nerves running through them. A toothache occurs when the nerves inside are exposed or damaged.

the synapse to the dendrites of the next neuron in line. These chemicals give the next neuron two choices. It can either increase or decrease the likelihood that the next neuron will send the impulse along. For example, if you go to the dentist to have a cavity filled, you will sometimes get an injection of medication that numbs your mouth. The numb feeling occurs because you have lost sensation in part of your mouth. That is because the medication blocks the nerve impulses that would otherwise make you feel the pain of having a cavity filled. You do not feel the pain because the nerve impulse does not travel from neuron to neuron to your brain.

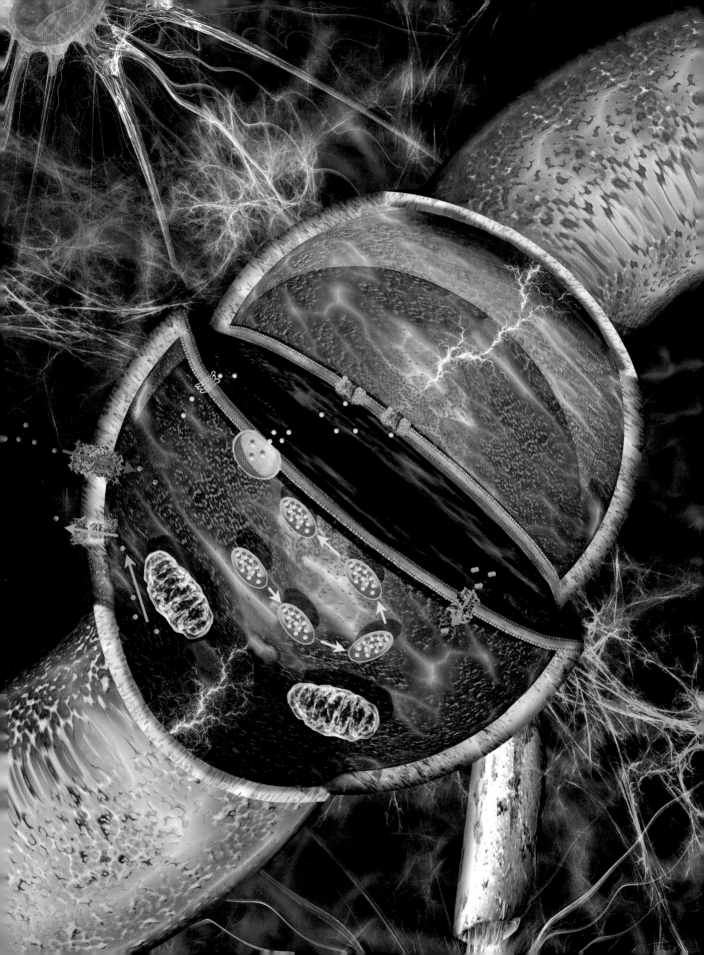

2

How Does the Nervous System Work?

The brain is what makes it possible for us to do all the things we do in our lives. It is also responsible for regulating our glands and organs. It receives, interprets, and responds to nerve impulses. It enables our five senses to give us the world in all its incredible richness and complexity.

Besides being in charge of our body's primary functions, the brain is a very sensitive organ. It is easily bruised or injured. Fortunately, it is enclosed in five layers of protection. The outermost layer is the skull. The next three layers are tough membranes called meninges.

Without the transmission of electrical and chemical signals between neurons, the nervous system would not function.

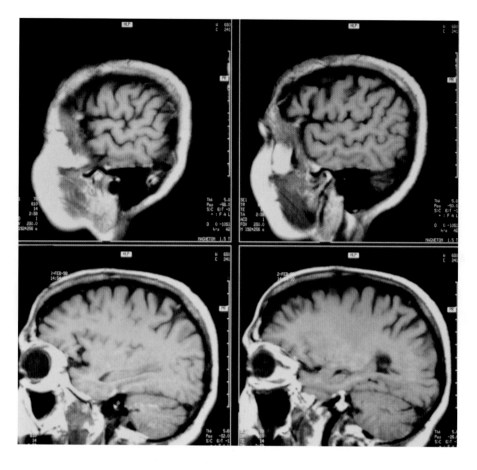

The fragile brain is protected by the hard and bony skull (white outline). Between the brain and skull are layers of meninges and cerebrospinal fluid that cushion the brain.

In the space between the second and third meninges, a layer of clear cerebrospinal fluid acts as a liquid cushion for added protection between the brain and the skull.

Before a child is born, the brain develops at a very fast rate. Each minute about 250,000 neurons are added. By the time a child is born, the brain has almost all of the neurons the person will need for the rest of his or her life. But the brain does not stop growing. By the age of two, the child's brain will be about 80 percent of the size of an adult brain. Much of the additional brain matter comes from specialized cells called glia or neuroglia. Glial cells are necessary for normal brain functions. They also support nerve cells in the brain and spinal cord by producing myelin, a protein-based substance that insulates nerve axons. This insulation acts as a protective covering that allow nerve impulses to travel more smoothly from neuron to neuron.

A healthy brain is like a smoothly functioning team. A football team, or any team for that matter, is made up of players with specific jobs

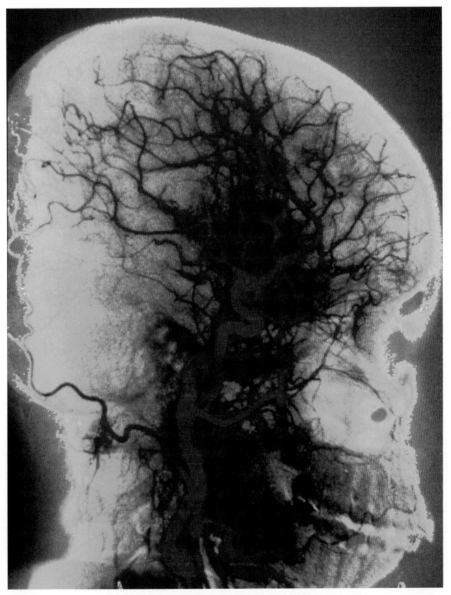

The nerves and tissues of the brain stay healthy and active because of the nutrients provided by the many blood vessels (red).

to do. When all the players are doing their job and working well with each other, the team is in good shape. It is the same way with the brain, which consists of different parts and structures. Each part of the brain has a specific structure and a unique set of functions to perform.

TWO HEMISPHERES

The brain has two halves, or hemispheres. The right hemisphere controls the left half of the body. The left hemisphere controls the right half of the body. Scientists used to think that the two hemispheres were extremely different in terms of their functions. But current research suggests the

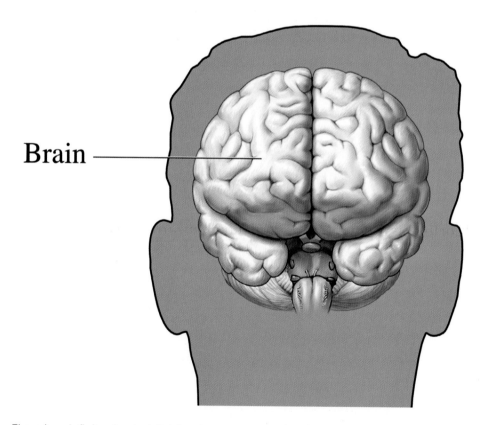

Brain

There is a definite physical division that creates two hemispheres, or halves, of the brain, but scientists continue to explore how these two halves are used.

differences may not be that huge. Still, these differences do exist, and may cause different styles of thinking or interpreting and processing information.

The left hemisphere is more oriented toward logical, rational thinking, the right hemisphere is more sensitive to colors, shapes, and sounds, and better able to recognize larger patterns. A student who is considered "left-brained" might do well in math and science. A student who is more "right-brained," on the other hand, might be more interested in creative or artistic pursuits. A "whole-brained" student would likely feel comfortable exercising both hemispheres of his brain.

The two halves of the brain are able to communicate with each other through the corpus callosum. The corpus callosum is a thick bundle of nerve fibers just above the brain stem.

THE CEREBRUM

The cerebrum is the largest part of the brain. It makes up about 85 percent of the brain's weight. The cerebrum's job is to handle our thoughts and feelings, our capacity for language and reasoning, and our performance of voluntary actions.

The outer covering of the cerebrum is called the cerebral cortex. The word "cortex" is from a Latin word which means "bark." The cortex itself looks somewhat like the grooved bark of a tree. In humans and in other highly evolved mammals, the cerebral cortex has many folds. The folding of the cerebral cortex produces many bumps and grooves. The bumps are called gyri (singular is gyrus). The grooves are sulci (singular is sulcus). The folds of the cerebral cortex increase the amount of cortex that can fit inside the skull.

In terms of evolution, the cerebral cortex is the most recent development. More folds mean a larger area of the brain is available

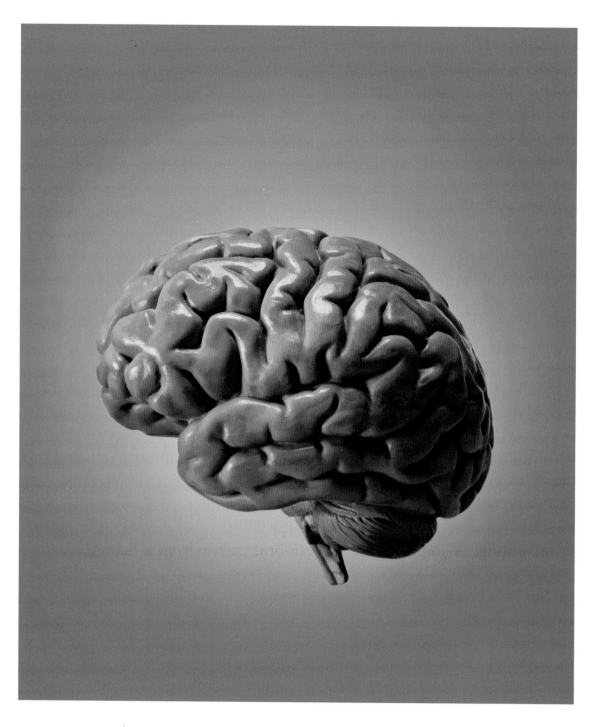

The shape and number of cerebral folds and grooves is unique to each person.

Anatomy and Functional Areas of the Brain

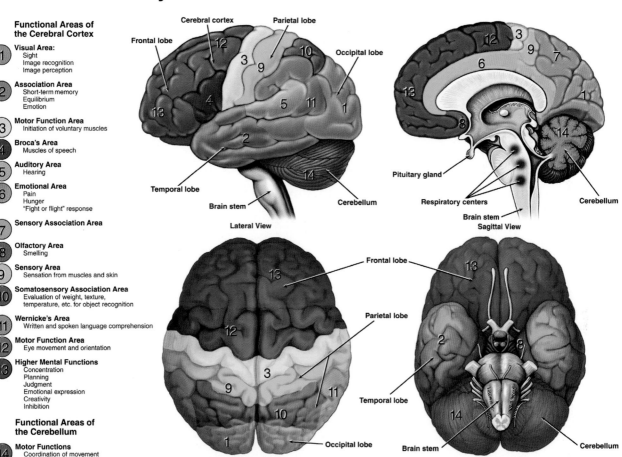

Functional Areas of the Cerebral Cortex

1 Visual Area:
Sight
Image recognition
Image perception

2 Association Area
Short-term memory
Equilibrium
Emotion

3 Motor Function Area
Initiation of voluntary muscles

4 Broca's Area
Muscles of speech

5 Auditory Area
Hearing

6 Emotional Area
Pain
Hunger
"Fight or flight" response

7 Sensory Association Area

8 Olfactory Area
Smelling

9 Sensory Area
Sensation from muscles and skin

10 Somatosensory Association Area
Evaluation of weight, texture,
temperature, etc. for object recognition

11 Wernicke's Area
Written and spoken language comprehension

12 Motor Function Area
Eye movement and orientation

13 Higher Mental Functions
Concentration
Planning
Judgment
Emotional expression
Creativity
Inhibition

Functional Areas of the Cerebellum

14 Motor Functions
Coordination of movement
Balance and equilibrium
Posture

Cerebral cortex
Parietal lobe
Frontal lobe
Occipital lobe
Temporal lobe
Brain stem
Cerebellum
Lateral View

Pituitary gland
Respiratory centers
Brain stem
Cerebellum
Sagittal View

Frontal lobe
Parietal lobe
Temporal lobe
Occipital lobe
Superior View

Frontal lobe
Brain stem
Cerebellum
Inferior View

for complex brain functions like thinking, reasoning, planning, and imagining. If you unfolded the cerebral cortex from a human brain, it would take up about 324 square inches, which is about the size of a page from a newspaper. The cortex has about 10 billion neurons with about 50 trillion synapses.

Each hemisphere of the cerebrum has four regions called lobes. Some of the longer grooves (sulci) mark the boundaries between the lobes. Each lobe has its own set of functions.

The frontal lobe handles speech, emotion, voluntary movements, and higher level functions like reasoning, planning, and judgment. The parietal lobe is involved with the sense of touch and the sensations of warmth and cold, and of pain. The occipital lobe manages our vision. The temporal lobe is mainly concerned with hearing.

THE CEREBELLUM

The cerebellum is the second-largest part of the brain. The name means "little brain" in Latin. It is an eighth of the size of the cerebrum. Like the cerebrum, the cerebellum has two hemispheres and a surrounding cortex.

The cerebellum is located in back of the brain, just below the cerebrum. The cerebellum is responsible for balance, movement, and coordination. It controls all of our voluntary movements. Without your "little brain," you would not be able to walk upright for very long. You also could not ice skate, windsurf, skateboard, or play any other sports.

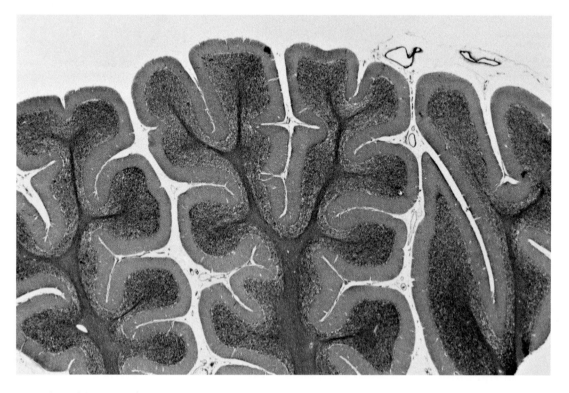

A section of the cerebellum.

THE STORY OF PHINEAS GAGE

In 1848 a man named Phineas Gage was working on a railroad construction crew in Vermont. One day a dynamite charge accidentally exploded, causing an iron bar to shoot through Phineas's head. The pointed end went in under Phineas's left cheekbone and flew out of the top of his head. The accident destroyed most of the frontal lobe of the left side of his brain.

Amazingly, Gage survived, but his personality underwent a dramatic change. Before the accident, people saw him as hard working, even-tempered, and sensible in all of his dealings. However, after the accident, his old friends hardly recognized him. He had become insensitive to others, unpredictable, and indecisive. The story of Phineas Gage gave scientists in the nineteenth century their first look into how different parts of the brain perform different functions and influence personality and emotion.

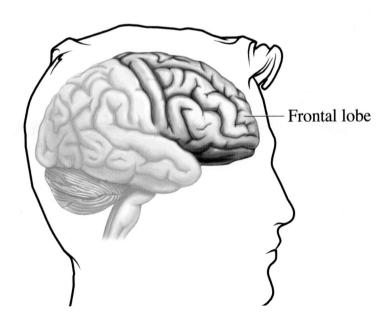

Frontal lobe

HOW DO WE LEARN?

When we are born, our brains have most of the neurons we will need for the rest of our lives. But many of these nerve cells are not connected with each other. As we learn new things, connections begin to form. As you kept repeating or practicing the new action, it became easier to do many them, often at the same time. This is because as you learned the new action and tried to do it, your nerve cells sent similar messages back and forth along the same routes in your brain. Gradually, your brain created connections. As these connections grew stronger, your skills improved. A similar process takes place whenever we are learning something new.

THE BRAIN STEM

The brain stem is sort of like the brain's personal postal service. It handles the millions of messages shuttling back and forth between the brain and the rest of the body. That is a pretty big job by itself, but it is not all that the brain stem does. This part of the brain also manages all the activities that keep us alive.

Thanks to the brain stem, we do not have to think about digesting our food, circulating our blood, or controlling our breathing. Imagine if we had to think about doing all of these things. There would be no time for anything else. The brain stem does it all for us by controlling our involuntary muscles. These include the muscles that keep our hearts beating and our stomachs and intestines converting food into energy and waste.

It is the brain stem that instructs your heart to pump more blood when you are running down the soccer field or chasing after the school bus. Like other parts of the brain, the brain stem is very complex and is made up of several smaller structures like the medulla oblongata, pons, and midbrain.

THE DIENCEPHALON

The diencephalon is located between the two cerebral hemispheres and above the midbrain of the brain stem. It includes two very important structures—the thalamus and the hypothalamus. The thalamus sends incoming sensory nerve impulses to appropriate regions of the brain where they are interpreted. The thalamus tells your brain, through the messages

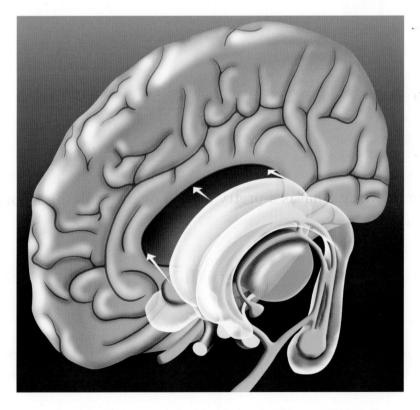

Some of the structures that make up the diencephalon include the hippocampus, thalamus, hypothalamus, and pituitary gland.

it sends, what you are seeing, hearing, tasting, smelling, and touching. It also receives outgoing messages from the cerebral cortex and passes this information to other parts of the brain or to the spinal cord.

The hypothalamus is only about the size of a pea. But for something so small, it has a very important role to play. Its major responsibility involves making sure your body's needs are taken care of. It tells you when you are hungry or thirsty, for example, and does its best to keep your body temperature within a normal range. When you are cold, the hypothalamus makes you shiver to raise your temperature. When you

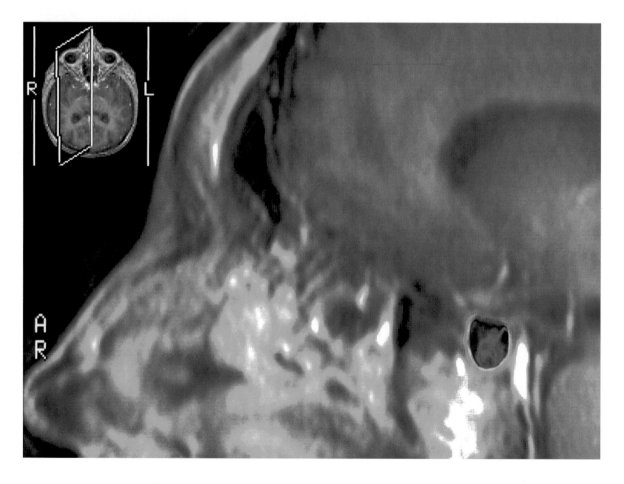

The pituitary gland (colored pink in this scan called an MRI) is often called the master gland because it sends out instructions to many glands and organs responsible for important life processes.

are overheated, it comes to your rescue once again by making you sweat in order to lower your body temperature. It also tells the blood vessels in your skin to expand so your blood can start to cool.

THE PITUITARY GLAND

Like the hypothalamus, the pituitary gland is small but important. The pituitary gland produces and releases special chemicals called hormones. These chemicals stimulate responses like "fight or flight" reactions to a dangerous or threatening situation. The pituitary gland also regulates the growth of your body and the many changes that occur as a child enters puberty and becomes an adult. The little gland also helps to manage your metabolism, which includes chemical reactions and processes that provide your body with nutrients and energy.

THE LIMBIC SYSTEM

Without emotions and feelings, we would only be partially human. Our emotional responses are forever changing as we deal with the many different situations and challenges that confront us every day. So where do our emotions come from? What is the source of our feelings?

Many scientists think the brain's limbic system holds the answer to these questions. This system is really the interplay between two structures of the brain—the hippocampus and the amygdala. The amygdala is where we feel different emotions in ourselves and perceive different emotions in other people. Located between the corpus callosum and the temporal lobe, the hippocampus resembles a tiny seahorse. It is important for memory and learning.

THE SPINAL CORD

Like the brain, the spinal cord is part of the central nervous system. It looks like a slender white cable, somewhat like the cable that a television uses. A television cable transmits audio and video signals from outside sources to the parts inside the television. In a similar way, the spinal cord carries other kinds of electrical signals to and from the brain. Sensory nerves carry incoming signals that tell your brain what you are experiencing at any given moment. Outgoing signals from the brain pass through the spinal cord and tell your muscles, glands, and organs what to do about this information.

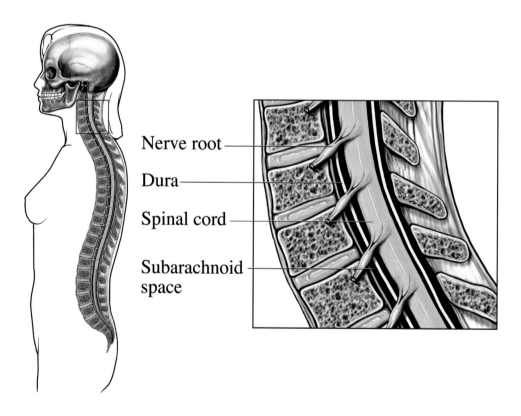

Nerve root

Dura

Spinal cord

Subarachnoid space

An illustration of a portion of the spinal cord shows the outermost meninges (the dura), the roots of the spinal nerves, and the subarachnoid space which is a cerebrospinal fluid-filled area between meninges.

If you put your hand too close to a flame, for instance, pain receptors in your hand send nerve impulses along neural pathways that extend up through the spinal cord to parts of your brain that recognize the sensation of pain. The brain responds by telling you to pull your hand to get away from the fire. In a person with a healthy nervous system, the entire process happens in the blink of an eye thanks to the work of your central and peripheral nervous systems.

In adults, the spinal cord is about 17 inches (43 cm) long in women and 18 inches (45 cm) in men. It weighs about 1 ounce (35 to 40 grams) and is about half an inch (1.27 cm) wide. The top of the spinal cord connects with the base of the brain at the brain stem. The lower end stops about two-thirds of the way down the spinal column.

The most important function of the spinal cord is to carry information to and from the brain. Because of its extreme sensitivity, the spinal cord must be protected from injury. Three tough membranes called meninges surround it. A layer of cerebrospinal fluid between the inner and middle membrane nourishes the spinal cord and serves as a shock absorber. The spinal cord resides in the spinal column, or spine, which is composed of thirty-three bones called vertebrae. Flexible discs of cartilage separate and cushion the vertebrae. This allows the spine to stretch and bend.

The entire spine has five distinct regions. The cervical or neck region has seven vertebrae. The cervical vertebrae are often referred to as C1 to C7. The thoracic or upper back region has twelve vertebrae (T1 to T12). The lumbar or lower back region has five vertebrae (L1 to L5). There are a total of nine fused vertebrae in the sacral and coccygeal regions. The sacral region is also called the sacrum. The coccygeal region at the base of the spine is also called the coccyx, or tailbone.

Like the spinal column, the spinal cord is divided into segments. These segments correspond to the different parts of the spine (cervical, thoracic, lumbar, and sacral). While the spine has thirty-three bones, the

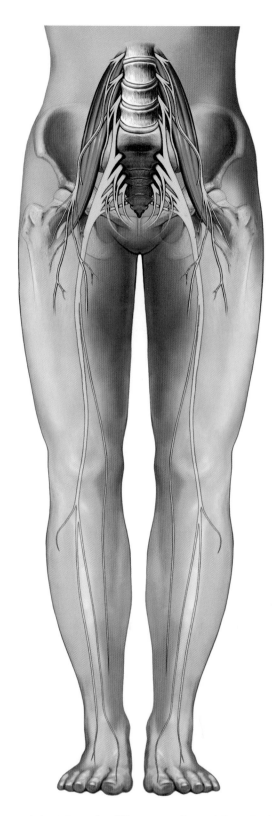

Pairs of spinal nerves jut out from the different sections of the spinal cord. This illustration shows the sacral nerves that exit the sacral part of the spine and travel down the legs.

SPINAL NERVES	THE AREAS OF THE BODY THAT THEY SERVE
Cervical spinal nerves	Back of the head, neck, shoulders, arms, hands, and diaphragm
Thoracic spinal nerves	Chest and parts of abdomen
Lumbar spinal nerves	Lower back and parts of thighs and legs
Sacral spinal nerves	Buttocks, most of legs and feet, anal and genital area

spinal cord has thirty-one pairs of spinal nerves. There is one pair for each segment of the spinal cord. These nerves reach out from the spinal cord to all parts of the body and carry impulses to and from the brain. They control the movement of our muscles and carry sensations from our body's five senses. They also regulate our body's production of various fluids.

The Gray and the White

Scientists also describe the spinal cord in terms of what it is made of. If you look at a cross-section of a spinal cord, you can see two kinds of matter. One kind is gray and the other is white. The gray matter resembles the wings of a butterfly. This is where nerve cell bodies are located. These neurons transmit messages between the spinal cord and the pairs of spinal nerves.

The white matter is made of axons, the extensions that carry impulses away from the nerve cell body. Most of the white matter is in the cervical region where numerous axons travel from the brain to the different segments of the spinal cord and from these segments up to the brain. The fewest number of axons is in the sacral region. So there is much less white matter in this region of the spinal cord.

THE FIVE SENSES

We need our senses in order to experience what is happening inside and outside our bodies. Without the nervous system, our senses would not work.

Touch

Our organs, muscles, and bones are contained in one big, washable, extra sensitive covering, we call skin. The skin is the largest organ in the human body. Sweat glands, hair follicles, blood vessels, and nerve endings are located in the skin. Unlike the other senses, the sense of touch is not limited to one area of the body. However, some parts are more sensitive than others. It all depends on how many receptors, or nerve endings are present in that area of skin.

An illustration of a cross-section of the skin shows the blood vessels and nerves that run through the inner layers.

The tongue, lips, hands, and fingertips are among the most sensitive areas. The face, neck, and feet are also extra sensitive to the sense of touch. Our skin contains an assortment of touch receptors. The most common ones are for pressure, pain, temperature, vibration, and movement. There are more nerve endings for pain than for any other type of touch receptor.

Without a sense of touch, we could not tell where our feet are when we walk. We would not know if something were hot or cold, wet or dry, soft or hard. We could not feel the keys on a piano or the keyboard of a computer. Our sense of touch enables us to find our way through the world around us, to handle objects, and coordinate our movements.

Nerve endings in the skin carry information to the spinal cord, which sends it to the brain. What happens after touch signals reach the brain? The brain decides what all these signals mean. Usually, the brain receives a wide range of signals at the same time. It quickly processes this information and tells you all the qualities of whatever you are touching. So if you are holding a hot, cooked potato, you know that in addition to being hot, the potato is round, has a dry covering, and is soft enough to squish in your hand.

Sight

Our eyes make it possible for us to see the world around us. Some neuroscientists think of the eye as an extension of the brain. For us to see the world in its many colors and shapes, our eyes must first absorb light.

Light rays pass through the pupil, which is the opening in the eye. Small muscles attached to the iris widen or narrow the pupil depending on how much light is available. Located behind the iris, the lens focuses the light. The lens directs the light to the back of the eye where the retina is located. The retina in each eye contains about 120 million rods and

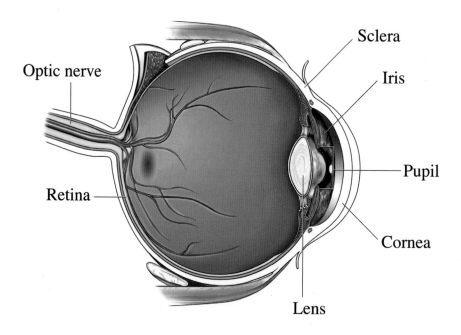

Axons bundle together to form the thick optic nerve at the back of the eyeball.

about 7 million cones. These tiny structures are light-sensitive neurons, or photoreceptors. Their job is to convert light into nerve impulses, which are then transmitted to the brain by way of the optic nerve.

Working together, the rods and cones in the retina change what we are looking at into nerve impulses. How do they do this? Molecules within each rod or cone are sensitive to particular wavelengths of light. When light strikes these molecules, they change their shape. This shape change triggers a chain reaction of events within the retina. In an instant, an electrical pulse is generated. The pulse travels down the axon of the rod or cone to the ganglion cells. The axons of ganglion cells form the optic nerve, which travels to the brain from the back of the eyeball and is made of about one million axons. The part of the brain that receives and processes these nerve signals is the occipital lobe of the cerebral cortex.

Because the lens turns images upside down on the retina, the brain needs to turn them right side up. It must also merge the two slightly different images coming from both eyes in order for us to see in three dimensions.

Hearing

The job of the ear is to collect sounds, change them into nerve signals, and funnel these signals to the brain where they become the music you listen to, the voice of a friend on the telephone, the familiar sounds of a plane passing overhead, a dog barking, or a car going by.

Sounds first enter the outer ear and travel through the ear canal to make the eardrum vibrate. These vibrations travel through the middle ear where they stimulate the ossicles, the smallest and most delicate bones in the human body. The ossicles relay sound vibrations to the oval window, a

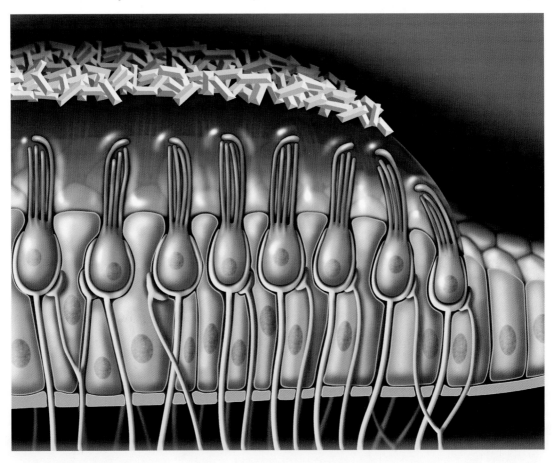

Sensory neurons (yellow) and motor neurons (green) receive and send messages coming from the hair cells (orange) in the inner ear.

KEEPING YOUR BALANCE

When we are born, our brains have most of the neurons we will need for Hearing is not the only job our ears do for us. They also help us keep our balance. Right above the cochlea in the inner ear there are three small loops called semicircular canals. The canals contain liquid and thousands of sensory hairs. Each time you move your head, the fluid in the canals moves, too. This movement causes the microscopic hairs inside the canals to move. The movement of the hairs produces nerve impulses that tell the brain the exact position of your head. Your brain then sends a message to your muscles. Knowing which muscles to move and when to move them keeps you from losing your balance and falling down.

Have you ever spun around and then stopped suddenly, or gotten off an amusement park ride that had you going in circles? Chances are you felt dizzy after the ride or the spinning ended. Your body has stopped moving. But the little hairs in your semicircular canals have not gotten the message yet. They think you are still moving. So does your brain. In fact, your brain is a bit confused. It does not know the position of your head. So you feel dizzy until the fluid in the semicircular canals settles down and you get your balance back.

thin layer of tissue at the entrance to the inner ear. From the oval window, vibrations travel to the inner ear where a small, fluid-filled structure called the cochlea is located. Vibrations cause liquid in the cochlea to move in a wavelike motion. This movement stimulates microscopic hairs inside the organ of Corti, a spiral structure within the cochlea. The movement of these hairs generates nerve impulses that travel to the brain along auditory nerves. Areas in the brain important for hearing translate these impulses into the sounds you hear and recognize.

Smell

You have the ability to smell because special sensory cells inside your nose can detect the chemicals that make up different odors. It does not take much for your nose to detect and identify odors. A few molecules floating in the air and drifting through your nostrils are enough to stimulate the sense of smell. The nostrils allow smells to reach the nasal cavity. The nasal cavity is a space in the back of your nose and in the middle of your face.

The roof of the nasal cavity has a specialized membrane known as the olfactory epithelium. This membrane contains millions of olfactory receptor cells. These smell receptors are not all the same, and different kinds can detect different odors. When odor molecules reach the nasal cavity, they dissolve in a layer of mucus, a slippery substance. Microscopic hairs attached to the smell receptors absorb the molecules and activate the receptor cells. When smell receptors are activated, electrical signals pulse along the olfactory nerve to the olfactory bulb. The olfactory bulb is under the front of your brain and just above the nasal cavity. Signals travel from the olfactory bulb to several different parts of your brain, including those that are involved with emotion and memory. One odor can activate several different kinds of receptors at the same time. It is up to the brain to figure out what these different combinations mean so you can tell whether you are smelling a fresh bouquet of flowers, for instance, or the repulsive odor of a skunk.

Taste

You might think your tongue is what lets you taste the sweetness of ice cream or the sourness of lemons. Actually, it is what is on your tongue that gives you the sense of taste. The tongue is covered with little bumps. These bumps are called papillae. Most of them are full of taste buds, which are responsible for all the tastes you experience. A person has about 10,000 taste buds. Each one contains between fifty to one hundred taste receptor cells. Microscopic hairs called microvilli protrude from each of these cells.

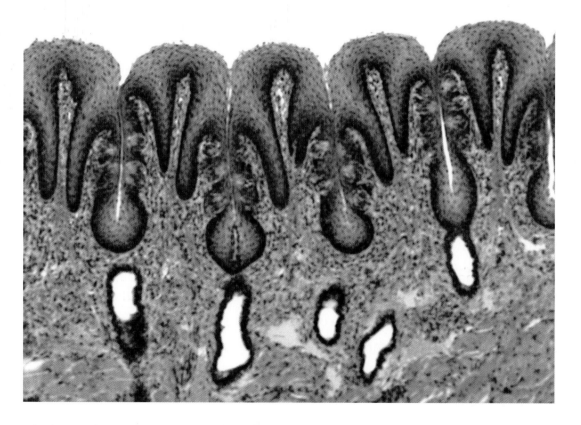

A microscopic look at papillae and taste buds.

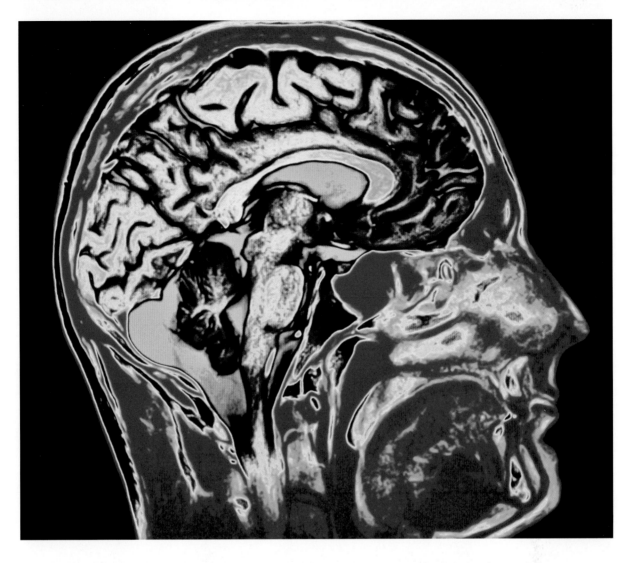

Scientists are continually learning more about how the brain processes the information carried through the complex network of nerves.

These hairs sample the foods in your saliva. They become activated and transmit nerve signals to your brain.

Two nerves deliver taste sensations to the brain from different parts of the tongue. These nerves, called cranial nerves, carry this information first to the brain stem. From there, it travels to the thalamus and then to the cerebral cortex. Like our experience of smell, the experience of taste also affects the limbic system, which is responsible for emotion and memory. As with smell, certain tastes have the power to trigger powerful memories and the feelings that go with them.

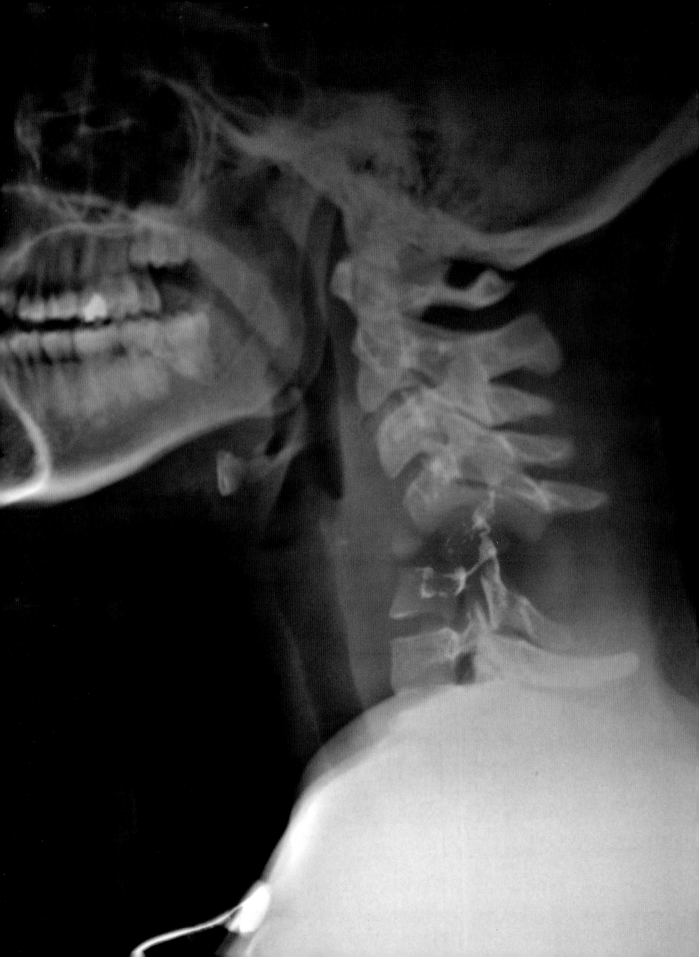

3

Diseases and Disorders

Many different things can affect the nervous system. Some problems are normal occurrences that everyone goes through at one time or another. However, there are a number of diseases and disorders that require careful observation and treatment by health professionals.

HEADACHES

Just about everyone has suffered from a headache at one time or another. Though it may seem like it, for nearly all headaches the problem is not that your brain actually hurts. The brain itself actually

A colored X ray shows a neck fracture, where the cervical vertebrae have broken (red), damaging the spinal cord.

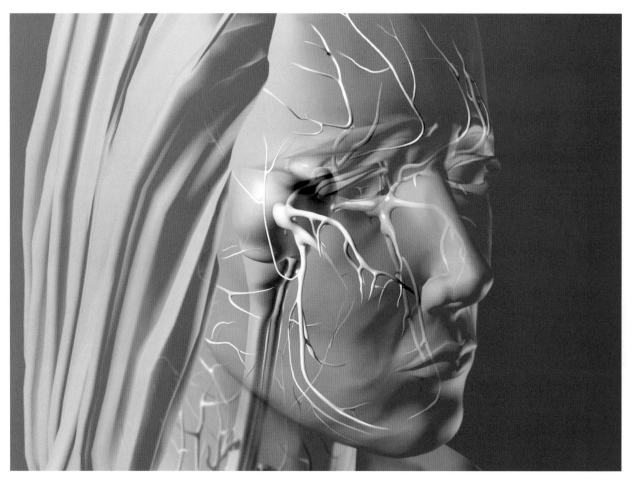

Many scientists believe that there are specific nerves—such as the trigeminal nerves in the face—involved in painful migraine headaches.

lacks pain-sensitive nerve cells. So while your brain can interpret pain from other parts of the body, it cannot sense pain in its own brain tissue.

Many headaches are caused by stress and tension, which causes the muscles and blood vessels in the head or neck to either enlarge or contract. This change puts pressure on nearby nerves, which send pain message to your brain. The pain you feel is located in these muscles as well as the blood vessels and nerves that cover your skull and neck.

Many doctors also believe that headaches can be caused by changes in hormones or other chemicals in the body. These changes can affect nerve activity and the way the brain controls the body's neurotransmitters, leading to headache pain. Certain foods can also cause changes in your body that bring on a headache. Strong emotions like excitement about an upcoming event, not getting enough sleep, staring too long at a computer screen, and even strong odors can also trigger headaches.

A migraine is less common than tension or stress headaches, but are usually a lot more painful. The pain from a migraine is much more intense than ordinary headaches. People who experience migraines feel tired, dizzy, have problems with their vision, or are nauseated, which means they feel like vomiting. Many doctors believe that migraines can be caused by changes in hormones and other chemical imbalances in the body.

For most headaches, including migraines, rest and correctly taking the right kind of medication can help ease the pain. But if headaches are frequent, constant, or extremely painful you should be checked by a neurologist. Neurologists are doctors who specialize in the nervous system. Sometimes frequent and painful headaches can be a symptom of a serious condition.

CONCUSSIONS

Concussions occur when the brain and its nerves are forcefully moved. Sometimes the brain knocks against the inside of the skull. This sudden jolt can affect how the brain and nerves perform. In some cases, it can lead to temporary unconsciousness. For children, playing soccer is a leading cause of concussions. Professional athletes like boxers and football players sometimes experience multiple concussions during their careers. These injuries can produce serious medical problems.

The typical symptoms of a mild concussion include nausea, dizziness, and headache. Severe concussions may result in unconsciousness, bleeding inside the head, and bruising of the brain. Whether mild or severe, a concussion should be treated immediately. A child who has experienced

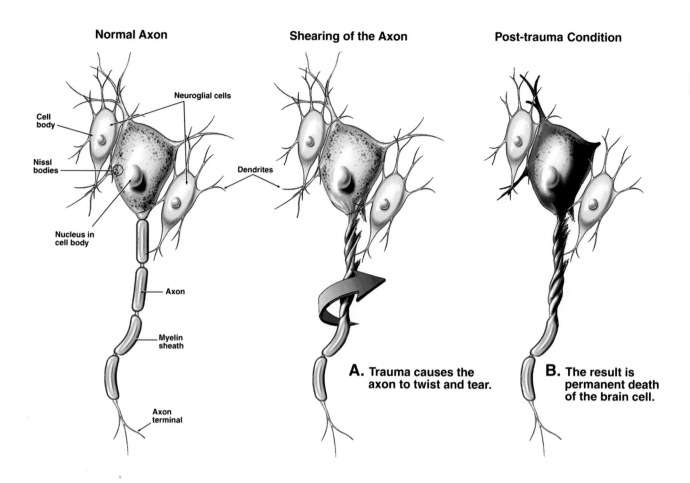

Normal Axon

Shearing of the Axon

Post-trauma Condition

Neuroglial cells

Cell body

Nissl bodies

Dendrites

Nucleus in cell body

Axon

Myelin sheath

Axon terminal

A. Trauma causes the axon to twist and tear.

B. The result is permanent death of the brain cell.

This illustration shows how a healthy brain neuron (left) can be damaged during a concussion (middle). The force of the concussion can cause the neuron's axon to twist and tear. When the axon is damaged it usually causes the neuron to die. If many brain neurons die, serious brain damage occurs.

a concussion should be examined by a doctor or taken to the emergency room if he is unconscious or having symptoms. The doctor will try to determine the severity of the injury and to see if memory and the ability to concentrate have been affected. The doctor will also test the patient's balance and coordination. If the doctor thinks the brain might have been bruised or is bleeding, a CT scan will be done. This is a special X ray that will show the doctor the condition of the brain. In most cases, a person who has experienced a mild concussion can go back to normal activities after a few days or weeks of taking it easy.

TRAUMATIC BRAIN INJURIES

Traumatic brain injuries are a form of concussion, but are much more severe. A traumatic brain injury, or TBI, is what happens when the brain itself is damaged from hitting a hard surface or having something pass through the skull and penetrate the brain. Major causes of TBI include car accidents, falls, sports injuries, and physical abuse.

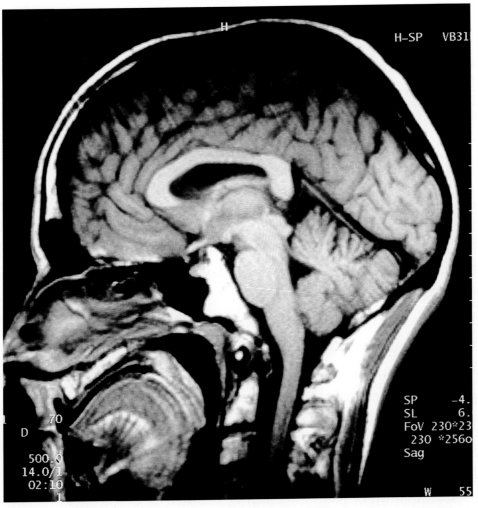

To check for traumatic brain injuries, doctors will often take X rays, scans, and run tests to check for damage to the brain.

TBI can produce a range of physical and mental changes depending on which areas of the brain are damaged. Damage to the frontal and temporal lobes of the brain, for instance, may result in problems with speech and language as well as with walking, balance, coordination, reasoning, memory, and even the ability to smell. TBI can also cause problems with thinking, paying attention, problem solving, judgment, behavior, seeing, hearing, and learning. The severity and duration of the symptoms depend on the how the trauma occured, the part of the brain that has been damaged, and the age and physical condition of the patient.

The symptoms of mild TBI include headache, confusion, brief unconsciousness, dizziness, blurred vision, ringing in the ears, fatigue, problems falling or staying asleep, and trouble concentrating. The symptoms of moderate to severe TBI can include convulsions or seizures, slurred speech, weakness or numbness, agitation, restlessness, repeated vomiting, loss of coordination, and the inability to awaken from sleep.

The initial damage caused by brain injury cannot be reversed. People with moderate to severe TBI should receive medical treatment as soon as possible. A team of doctors will first stabilize the patient to prevent further injury. They will also make sure there is enough oxygen and blood getting to the brain and the rest of the body, and control the patient's blood pressure. With the help of an imaging test, they can determine the exact location and extent of brain injury. Rehabilitation may include a range of therapies.

About 200,000 Americans die each year from TBI. About 500,000 people who have suffered brain trauma have to be hospitalized and may have long-term problems living on their own. This is why it is very important to protect your body and your brain by being safe and avoiding risky activities. And if a head injury occurs it is very important to go to a doctor or emergency room as soon as possible.

SPINAL CORD INJURIES

Most spinal cord injuries happen when the hard, protective vertebrae of the spinal column are crushed or pushed out of place from a sudden blow or fall. Pieces of bone, disc fragments, or torn ligaments then cut into or bruise the spinal cord. Only in a small number of cases, the spinal cord is actually cut into two parts.

In most instances, crushed vertebrae damage the nerve axons that relay messages to and from the brain and the rest of the body. The damage can be mild or severe depending on how many axons are destroyed from the injury. People who have experienced mild injuries to their spinal cord may fully recover.

Incomplete spinal cord injuries are those in which the person still has some feeling and movement below the injury. People with complete spinal cord injuries lose all feeling and are totally paralyzed below the point of the injury. Spinal cord injuries usually result in other medical problems. The person will likely have constant pain and difficulty going to the bathroom. He or she may also develop problems with his heart and lungs. People with spinal cord injuries rely on different kinds of physical rehabilitation programs to manage their disabilities.

Researchers are also experimenting with new medications and looking for ways to re-grow damaged axons. Making sure these new axons connect with the appropriate nerve cells is an important part of this work. Only then will it be possible to restore sensation and movement.

Stem cell research is another promising direction in the treatment of spinal cord injuries. Neurons in the brain or spinal cord are not able to repair or replace themselves after being injured. But it might be possible to transplant other kinds of cells into the injured area and get them to perform like neurons. Stem cells are cells in the human embryo that have not yet begun to form specific kinds of cells, like red blood cells or bone

Normal Anatomy

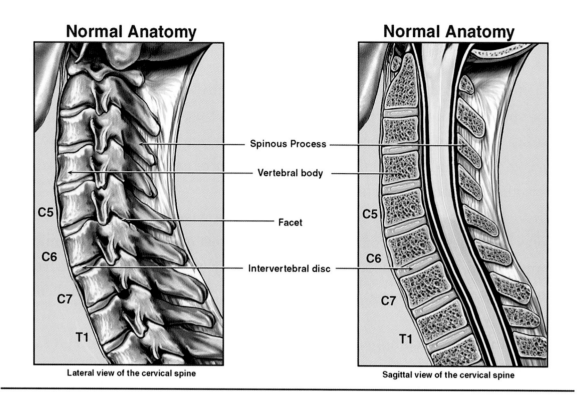

Spinous Process

Vertebral body

C5

Facet

C6

Intervertebral disc

C7

T1

Lateral view of the cervical spine

Normal Anatomy

C5

C6

C7

T1

Sagittal view of the cervical spine

Post-accident Condition

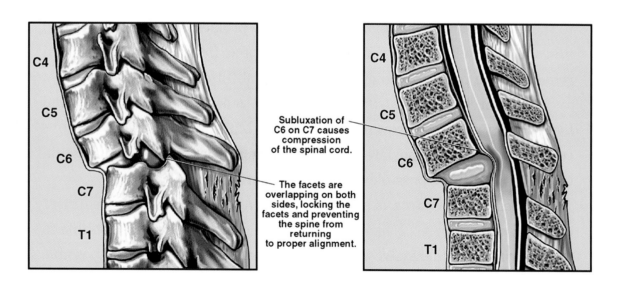

C4

C5

C6

C7

T1

Post-accident Condition

C4

Subluxation of C6 on C7 causes compression of the spinal cord.

C5

The facets are overlapping on both sides, locking the facets and preventing the spine from returning to proper alignment.

C6

C7

T1

These illustrations show how a healthy spinal cord (top) can be damaged when the vertebrae of the spine are forced out of place (bottom). As a result, the spinal cord can be compressed, bruised, or even severed.

cells. One research goal is to stimulate stems cells from embryos to grow into nerve cells rather than some other kind of cell, and then transplant them into the injured spinal area.

Stem cell research is a very controversial topic. Despite the potential benefits that using stem cells may yield, many people are opposed to stem cell research because it involves creating and then killing the human embryos that have provided stem cells.

MULTIPLE SCLEROSIS

Multiple sclerosis, or MS, is a disease of the nervous system. It is usually not fatal, but it can be very disabling. Multiple sclerosis is caused by the body's immune system. Instead of defending the body from invading bacteria or viruses, the immune system attacks itself. In the case of multiple sclerosis, the immune system treats the myelin around nerve cells as a foreign substance. It causes inflammation which may eventually destroy the myelin.

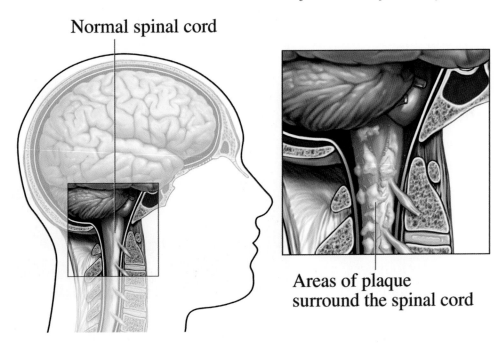

Normal spinal cord

Areas of plaque surround the spinal cord

When the myelin sheath is damaged by multiple sclerosis, plaque and scar tissue may build up, which interferes with transmitting impulses and messages.

As the myelin breaks down, nerve impulses are no longer transmitted the way they should be.

When this happens, a person with multiple sclerosis may have difficulty keeping his or her balance and coordination. If the optic nerve is affected, the person may have trouble seeing. Scientists do not know the exact cause of multiple sclerosis. A person's genetic make up and factors in the environment may trigger the onset of this disease. Though no cure presently exists, a number of different therapies and medications are used to help with the symptoms of Multiple sclerosis.

EPILEPSY

Epilepsy is a fairly common disease of the nervous system. About 1 in every 100 to 200 people has some form of epilepsy. During an epileptic seizure, the brain's normal electrical activity undergoes a drastic and sudden change. As a result, the brain is temporarily unable to process incoming signals and to control skeletal muscles. The person having the seizure may lose consciousness and experience violent shaking as the muscles involuntarily contract.

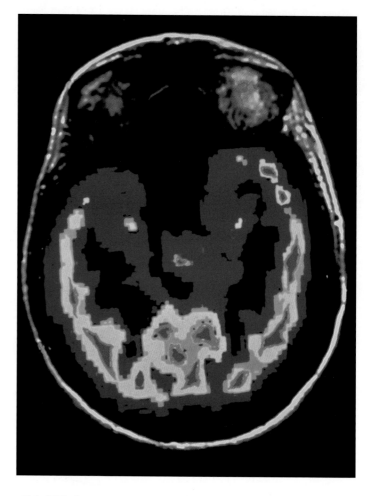

This MRI shows the increased activity in specific parts of the brain during an epileptic seizure. Pinpointing these affected areas can often help doctors develop a course of treatment for the patient.

SEIZURE-ASSISTANCE DOGS

Some people can tell when they are about to have an epileptic seizure. They may feel dizzy or nauseous or experience other early warning signs, which gives them time to protect themselves from the effects of a seizure. These warning signs are known as an aura.

Some dogs can be trained to help someone having an epileptic seizure. Such dogs can learn to activate an alarm system, alert family members, or even lie next to the person to prevent injury. It is also possible to train some dogs to sense when a person is going to have a seizure. When the training is effective, the dogs develop different ways of alerting the person, from pawing in a special way to getting close to the person and barking.

There are several different types of epilepsy, each one with its own set of symptoms. Brain injuries sometimes cause epileptic seizures, but in most people, doctors do not know what causes the epilepsy. However, doctors can identify certain triggers that can cause epileptic seizures. People with epilepsy can learn to avoid these triggers and take special medication that can prevent seizures.

STROKE

Stroke is the third leading cause of death in the United States after cancer and heart disease. Each year about 700,000 Americans have a stroke, according to the National Institute of Neurological Disorders and Stroke. Strokes happen when blood flow to the brain is suddenly stopped. The warning signs that usually precede a stroke are sudden weakness or numbness on one side of the body, loss of vision, often in one eye, difficulty speaking, severe headache, and dizziness.

There are two kinds of stroke. One kind, called hemorrhagic stroke, occurs when a blood vessel bursts in the brain. The more common kind is an ischemic stroke, which is responsible for about 80 percent of all strokes. An ischemic stroke happens when a blood vessel in the brain or

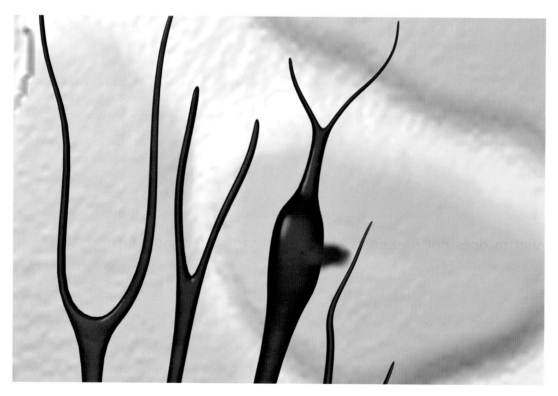

A hemorrhagic stroke occurs when a blood vessel bursts in the brain.

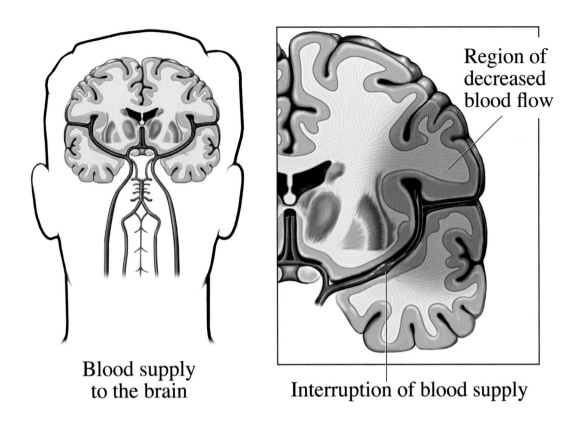

Region of decreased blood flow

Blood supply to the brain

Interruption of blood supply

A blockage in a blood vessel can cause an ischemic stroke. Without enough blood, brain cells will die.

neck becomes blocked. The blockage is caused by a blood clot or by the constriction of a blood vessel. The blood clot may have formed inside the blood vessel or traveled from some other part of the body.

Arteries are blood vessels that carry oxygen-rich blood to all parts of the body. Our brains use about 20 percent of this oxygen. During a stroke, the brain loses its supply of oxygen as well as essential nutrients carried in blood. As a result, neurons in the brain start to die. If the stroke victim does not die, he or she is likely to suffer some form of disability, including paralysis or speech impairment.

For strokes caused by clots, a drug called Activase or t-PA has been effective in dissolving some blood clots in the carotid artery. But it must be administered within 3 hours from the time of the stroke. To improve the effectiveness of Activase, doctors are using it along with ultrasound vibrations to break up and then dissolve the clot.

Recovery from a stroke depends on the overall health of the patient, the extent of the brain damage, and the type of treatment. Surgery, drugs, and physical and occupational therapy are the most common treatments for stroke. Doctors often prescribe regular exercise and a healthy diet to help their patients reduce blood pressure and cholesterol. Both high blood pressure and high cholesterol levels increase the chances of stroke. Physical therapy can help restore movement and speech, and occupational therapy helps stroke victims manage basic activities like getting dressed and performing other activities.

ALZHEIMER'S DISEASE

As people get older, their thinking may slow down and their memory may become weak. These changes are part of the normal aging process. But there are much more serious changes that happen in the case of Alzheimer's disease. This disorder of the brain is a form of dementia, which involves severe mental confusion, memory loss, and other major changes in how a person thinks and acts.

The German physician Alois Alzheimer first diagnosed Alzheimer's in 1906. He had been treating a fifty-one-year-old woman who had shown some very disturbing symptoms. After her death, Dr. Alzheimer looked at her brain and observed that the woman's cerebral cortex had actually shrunk. Using a microscope to examine samples of her brain, he saw deposits of fat in her blood vessels and many dead brain cells.

Thanks to Dr. Alzheimer's work and a lot of research that has been performed since, scientists now understand that this disease involves the loss of brain tissue and the death of irreplaceable nerve cells in the brain. The process only gets worse over time. As the brain shrinks due to tissue loss and nerve cell death, the person's mental abilities become severely reduced. The cerebral cortex is the region most damaged by Alzheimer's.

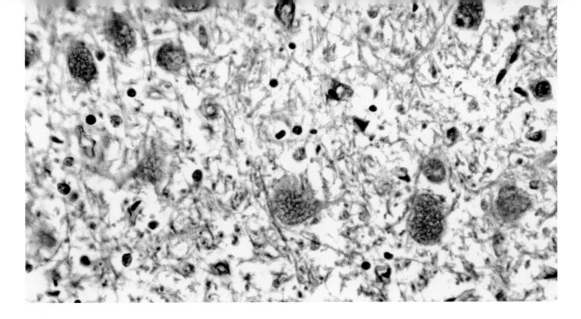

The plaques and tangles from a brain affected by Alzheimer's Disease are shown here as dark areas. These plaques and tangles interfere with brain activity, causing the symptoms of the disease.

This region is involved with thinking, planning, and remembering. The hippocampus, a part of the cortex where new memories are formed, is also affected by Alzheimer's.

In the last few decades, scientists have learned a great deal about this disease. Although they still do not understand what causes nerve cell death in the brain, their research has turned up two likely reasons— plaques and tangles. Plaques are a kind of protein that builds up between nerve cells. Tangles are another kind of protein that accumulates inside of dead and dying nerve cells. These plaques and tangles interfere with normal nerve activity, leading to problems with the nervous system.

Various kinds of treatments may slow down the process of nerve cell death and relieve some of the symptoms. Usually, doctors prescribe medications to deal with changes in thinking, language, and memory. But other kinds of changes may require a combination of drugs and non-drug treatments. For example, someone with Alzheimer's may become very restless or angry. A non-drug approach might involve keeping the person in a calm, stress-free environment to help him or her deal with the anxiety and frustration of the disease. There is no cure for Alzheimer's, but researchers hope to find one.

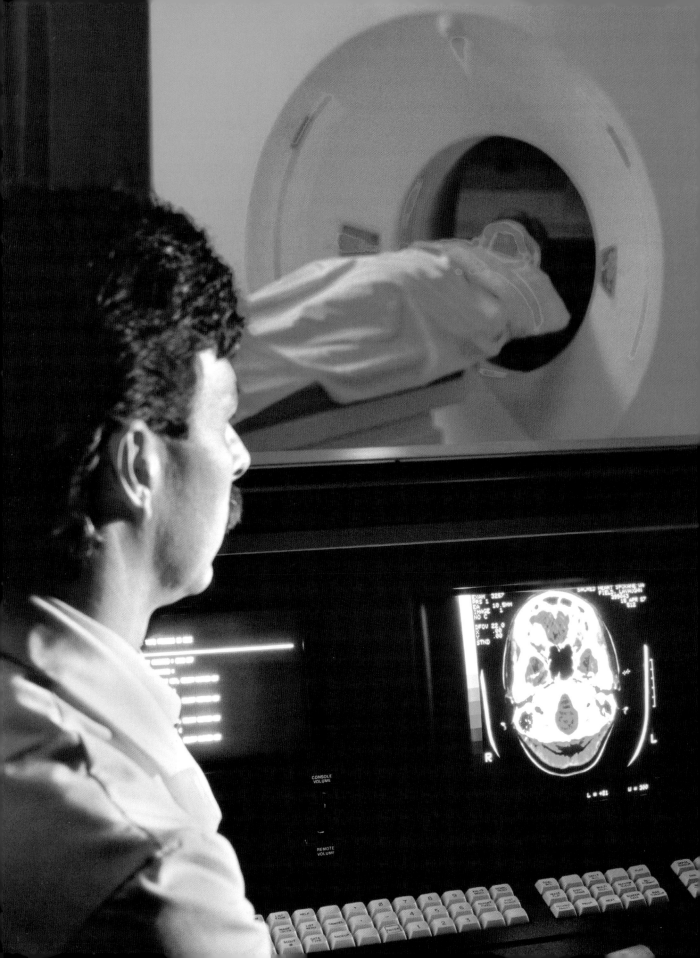

4

A Healthy Nervous System

hile certain diseases or disorders of the nervous system may be unavoidable, there are some things you can do to increase our chances of living a long and healthy life. Making sensible and responsible choices can help prevent damage to your nervous system.

PHYSICAL SAFETY

Your skull provides your brain with a hard casing that prevents some injuries, but you should still be careful when you participate in certain activities. Whenever you ride a bike or a skateboard, or go rollerblading,

By using technology like magnetic resonance imaging (MRI), doctors can diagnose many different brain disorders or diseases. Sometimes these scans can even help predict or prevent serious nervous system issues.

Helmets and other safety gear can help protect your body from serious damage.

you should always wear a helmet. If you fall, a helmet can help prevent concussions and fractures—or cracks—in your skull. Other safety gear, such as pads sleeves and long pant legs can help protect your skin and the delicate nerves beneath.

Be sure to wear the proper protective equipment when taking part in such contact sports as soccer, football, kickboxing, and martial arts. Each year hundreds of thousands of people suffer concussions while playing sports.

Always wear your seat belt when you ride in a car and never ride in the trunk, in the bed of a pickup truck, or on someone's lap. The seat belt is designed to keep you safe and anchored in case of an accident. Motor vehicle accidents are responsible for nearly half of all brain injuries. Concussions and spinal cord injuries can also result from car accidents.

If you like to dive into pools, lakes, or any body of water, you must make sure that the water is deep enough for diving. You should also look out for hidden objects below, such as rocks or tree trunks. If you dive into a body of water that is too shallow, or if your head crashes into a rock or other hard surface, you can be seriously hurt. You can crack your skull, damage your brain, get a concussion, or damage your spinal cord. Every year many people become paralyzed or die from diving accidents.

CHEMICAL SAFETY

Chemicals that enter your body can damage your nervous system. Dangerous chemicals can destroy nerve cells and interfere with the electrochemical transmissions. Overusing or improperly taking medication can cause these problems. Illegal drugs also damage your brain and nerves.

Chemicals found in certain household products can also harm you. Always follow the safety instructions on the products' labels. Use gloves

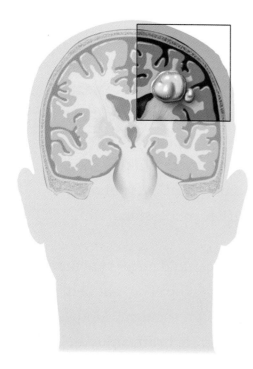
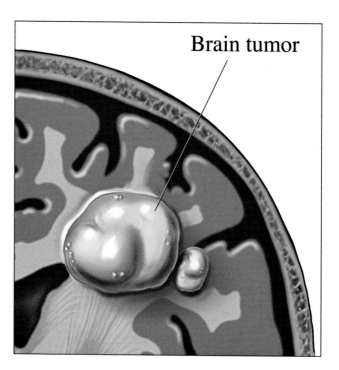

Brain tumor

Exposure to dangerous chemicals has been found to cause cancer, or an overgrowth of harmful cells in the body. Masses of these cells, called tumors, can form in many different parts of the body, including the brain.

and protective gear when necessary. Also make sure that there is proper ventilation so that you are not breathing in too many dangerous fumes.

A HEALTHY DIET

Our brains, like the rest of our bodies, need energy. We get this energy by eating carbohydrates, which are converted to glucose. Glucose is found in the body as blood sugar. Foods rich in carbohydrates include bread, pasta, rice, potatoes, sweets, and cereals. However, too many carbohydrates in our diets can cause weight gain and a rapid increase in our blood sugar level. High blood sugar levels can cause many different health issues.

Nutritionists usually recommend diets that contain complex, fiber-rich carbohydrates that take longer to metabolize, or break down, in the digestive system. This means that they can provide the body with a steady source of blood sugar. Foods that are a good source of healthy carbohydrates are fruit, vegetables, and legumes like beans, peas, and lentils.

We also need to eat the right amounts of vitamins, minerals, proteins, and fats to help our brains function properly. Proteins are composed of amino acids. Amino acids, in turn, are essential to the production of neurotransmitters. An imbalance in the supply of amino acids to the brain and central nervous system can produce a range of mental disorders.

Serotonin, for example, is a neurotransmitter produced from the amino acid tryptophan. Serotonin helps control appetite. It is also important in regulating moods. Nutritional studies show that if your diet does not have enough tryptophan, then your body will be unable to manufacture

Eating healthy amounts of nutritious food is important for your overall health. Some studies have shown that having a healthy diet can help maintain and improve your nerve functions.

enough serotonin. Low levels of serotonin can result in depression, sleep disorders, and anxiety. Nearly all proteins contain tryptophan, but foods that are especially good sources include red meat, dairy products, nuts, seeds, bananas, tuna, shrimp, and turkey. Proteins like milk, eggs, fish, and dairy products contain all of the essential amino acids necessary for a healthy nervous system.

Vitamins

In addition to proteins, our brain and nervous system also need B vitamins. The three most important B vitamins are thiaminee (B1), riboflavin (B2), and niacin (B3). A thiamine deficiency can cause memory loss, convulsions, and even paralysis. Fortunately, most people get enough thiamine in their diet. However, alcoholism and using some medications can lead to thiamine deficiency. Good sources of this vitamin are unrefined cereals and grains like brown rice and whole wheat, and nuts and legumes.

A diet that does not have enough niacin may cause depression and anxiety. Severe niacin deficiency has been known to cause dementia and even death. But this condition is rare. The amino acid tryptophan allows the body to make its own niacin. Proteins like meat and dairy products are excellent sources of this amino acid. Unrefined cereals and grains also provide niacin in addition to tryptophan.

Low amounts of riboflavin can interfere with the normal development of infants and children. In adults, alcoholism and anorexia, which is an eating disorder, can also cause a deficiency in riboflavin. A diet without enough riboflavin might not directly damage the nervous system, but it can lead to anemia, which is a blood disorder. Anemia can interfere with proper nervous system functions. Sources of riboflavin include dairy products, meat, poultry, fish, eggs, vegetables like spinach and broccoli, and cereals and breads fortified with B2.

Minerals

We need a wide variety of minerals in our diet in order to stay healthy. But two minerals—iron and iodine—are especially important for a healthy nervous system. Iron is used to make hemoglobin, a protein in red blood cells that carries oxygen to all parts of our body. Without oxygen, cells in the body will die. The billions of neurons in the brain use about 20 percent of the oxygen in blood. An iron-deficient diet causes anemia, and anemia can deprive the brain of the oxygen it needs. This can lead to serious brain and nervous system damage, especially in children during the first two years of life when their brains are still developing.

Older children can also experience iron deficiency. Symptoms may include tiredness, irritability, and difficulty concentrating. Foods that provide rich sources of iron are red meat, poultry, egg yolk, fish, dried fruit, and iron-fortified cereals.

At one time, too little iodine in the diet was a major cause of brain damage. Babies whose mothers had not eaten enough iodine were likely to have stunted bodies and impaired mental development. Nowadays, iodine has been added to ordinary table salt, which is included in most foods, so iodine deficiency is not very common. Food sources of iodine include seafood and leafy green vegetables.

EXERCISE

Exercise is good for you for many reasons. It makes your muscles strong. It helps you become more coordinated, and it can make you feel more confident in yourself. If you are overweight, getting regular amounts of exercise can help you lose weight. If too much homework is making you feel stressed out, then a good workout might make you feel better. In many

Exercise is good for many of your body systems. It keeps the muscles and bones strong, helps improve your blood flow, and helps you maintain a healthy weight. Your nervous system is affected by all of these things.

cases, intense physical activity can prompt the brain to release endorphins, which are chemicals that make you feel good.

The National Association for Sports and Physical Education recommends getting at least one hour of physical activity every day. This can be accomplished in one, 60-minute workout or in smaller sessions of 15 minutes or more throughout the day. Workouts should be adjusted based on how much you can safely do. If you are not used to working out a lot, you should start slowly and work your way up to longer workout sessions. Doing too much too quickly can injure muscles and cause a lot of pain.

Taking part in sports can be a healthy way to exercise. But that is not the only way to get the exercise you need. Swimming, hiking, going for brisk walks, or taking a bike ride can help you stay healthy. Walking or running with a dog, or even taking the stairs instead of the escalator or elevator can help.

Giving Your Brain a Workout

Exercising your brain is as important as exercising the muscles in your body. Since neurons appear to make new connections every time something

Studies have shown that people of all ages can keep their brains active and healthy by reading, doing puzzles, and performing other problem-solving activities.

new is learned, it is important to always try to learn new things. It is also important to maintain the neural connections that you have already formed. Reading, writing, doing puzzles, and problem solving appear to help keep the brain healthy.

SLEEP

Like exercise, sleep is necessary for maintaining health. Sleep gives our bodies a chance to re-energize so we are ready to meet the next day's challenges. Some scientists think that when we sleep many types of cells—including nerve cells—are able to repair themselves after all the hard work they have done during the day. When we do not get enough sleep, neurons become so overworked and worn out they can no longer do their job properly.

Sleep is also necessary in order to keep the mind in good working order. Getting enough sleep can help with your concentration and problem solving skills. Children between the ages of five and twelve need about ten or eleven hours of deep, restful sleep every night. Younger children need more sleep. Older adults tend to need less.

VISIT YOUR DOCTOR

Everyone should have regular checkups with their doctors. A doctor can help to monitor overall health and answer any questions you may have about staying healthy. Most doctors also perform routine exams and tests that can diagnose, or detect, any health issues that may be developing.

If you are having frequent or severe headaches or other problems with your nervous system, you should get checked out by a doctor as soon as possible. He or she might recommend that you visit a neurologist for special tests. A neurologist can usually determine what the problem is and how best to treat it. Early detection and treatment can make a huge difference when dealing with nervous system problems. Practicing a healthy lifestyle, knowing enough about your body, watching for warning signs, and then discussing any issues with a health professional can help you—and your nervous system—stay in good working order.

Glossary

action potential—Neurons send messages through electrochemical changes that occur along an axon. An action potential is an exchange of electrically charged chemicals like potassium and sodium across the membrane of an axon. This exchange allows a nerve impulse to travel to the next neuron in line.

afferent neurons—Nerves that carry electrical signals toward the brain and spinal column from other parts of the body.

amino acids—These are the chemical building blocks of proteins. Some amino acids are manufactured by the body, while others need to come from food, drinks, and dietary supplements.

amygdala—An almond-shaped structure in each hemisphere of the brain that appears to be the center of emotions, especially fear and the physical sensations that come with feeling afraid.

anemia—A shortage of red blood cells in the blood or an inadequate supply of hemoglobin, a blood protein that carries oxygen to the cells. Someone with anemia is likely to feel weak and lacking energy.

autonomic nervous system—The part of the nervous system responsible for regulating heartbeat and other involuntary actions.

axons—Extensions of nerves that carry nerve impulses away from the nerve cell and toward nearby neurons.

dementia—A mental condition characterized by confusion, disordered thinking, and memory loss.

dendrites—Branch-like extensions of nerve cells that receive nerve impulses from nearby axons of other nerve cells.

efferent neurons—Nerves that carry electrical signals away from the brain and spinal column toward other parts of the body.

embryo—A human offspring in the very early stages of development within its mother's womb.

ganglion cells—Types of neurons in the retina that carry visual information from the retina to the brain. Axons of these cells form the optic nerve.

hemoglobin—An iron-rich protein found in red blood cells. This protein carries oxygen from the lungs to cells in the body.

hemorrhagic stroke—A type of stroke in which a blood vessel in the brain bursts.

hippocampus—A structure in the brain that plays an important role in the formation of memories.

hormones—Chemicals produced by glands in the body. Hormones are important in regulating certain physical processes.

hypothalamus—About the size of a pea, this brain structure is responsible for process such as making sure the body's needs are met and maintaining normal body temperature.

interneurons—Nerve cells that send information between sensory and motor neurons. These are mostly located in the brain and spinal cord.

ischemic stroke—A type of stroke in which an artery in the brain or neck becomes blocked. Most strokes are ischemic strokes.

limbic system—A network of structures below the cerebral cortex that controls behaviors necessary for life. The limbic system includes the amygdala and the hippocampus, which are closely associated with emotion, memory, and learning. .

meninges—Tough layers of tissue that cover and protect the brain and the spinal cord.

metabolism—The combined interactions of all the chemical processes that provide the body with the energy and nutrients it needs to stay alive.

microvilli—Microscopic hair cells in the taste buds that sample food chemicals in the saliva and transmit nerve impulses to the brain.

myelin—A whitish substance made of protein and fats. Myelin coats the axons of nerve cells and facilitates the transmission of nerve impulses.

nerves—Bundles and bands of nervous tissue that connect the nervous system with organs and conduct nervous impulses.

neurologist—A doctor who specializes in the nervous system and related diseases and disorders.

neurons—Nerve cells.

neurotransmitters—Chemicals stored in nerve cells that carry nerve impulse across a synapse to another neuron or a muscle.

pituitary gland —Also called the "master gland," it is about the size of a pea and is located right below the hypothalamus in the brain. The hypothalamus tells the pituitary which hormones to release.

plaques—Protein build-ups around and inside brain neurons that appear to disrupt the normal functioning of neurons.

sensory receptors—Nerve endings that respond to stimuli like touch, pressure, heat, or pain and transmit nerve impulses in the form of electrical signals to the central nervous system.

serotonin—A neurotransmitter that helps control appetite and is important in regulating mood.

somatic nervous system—A part of the nervous system responsible for the voluntary actions of our muscles.

synapse—The space or gap between the end of a neuron's axon and the dendrites of a nearby neuron.

thalamus—A structure within the brain that sends incoming sensory nerve impulses to the brain and relays outgoing messages from the cerebral cortex to other parts of the brain or to the spinal cord.

Find Out More

Books

Aamodt, Sandra and Wang, Sam. *Welcome to Your Brain*. New York, New York: Bloomsbury, 2008.

Bjorklund, Ruth. *Epilepsy*. New York: Marshall Cavendish Benchmark, 2007.

Brill, Marlene Targ. *Multiple Sclerosis*. New York: Marshall Cavendish Benchmark, 2008.

Evans-Martin, Fay F. *The Nervous System*. Philadelphia, PA: Chelsea House Publishers, 2005.

Klosterman, Lorrie. *Meningitis*. New York: Marshall Cavendish Benchmark, 2007.

Newquist, H.P. *The Great Brain Book: An Inside Look at the Inside of Your Head*. New York: Scholastic, 2005.

Petreycik, Rick. *Headaches*. New York: Marshall Cavendish Benchmark, 2007.

Seymour, Simon. *The Brain: Our Nervous System*. New York, New York: Morrow Junior Books (Collins), 2006.

Websites

Brain and Nervous System
http://kidshealth.org/teen/your_body/body_basics/brain_nervous_system.
html

Brainteasers, Puzzles & Riddles—National Institute of Environmental
Health Sciences
http://kidshealth.org/kid/health_problems/heart/cystic_fibrosis.html

Epilepsy for Kids
http://www.epilepsy.com/KIDS/KIDS

Human Anatomy—The Nervous System
http://www.bbc.co.uk/science/humanbody/body/factfiles/nervous_anatomy.
shtml

Inside the Teenage Brain
http://www.pbs.org/wgbh/pages/frontline/shows/teenbrain

Neuroscience For Kids
http://faculty.washington.edu/chudler/introb.html

Overview of the Nervous System
http://quest.arc.nasa.gov/neuron/background/nervsys.html

Your Gross and Cool Body: Nervous System
http://yucky.discovery.com/noflash/body/pg000136.html

Index

About the Author

When George Capaccio was about twelve years old, he put together a plastic model called "The Invisible Man." It came with different parts for the different systems in the human body. Putting the "Invisible Man" together gave him his first big lesson in just how complex our bodies are—especially the nervous system. Now he has written a book about this fascinating subject. George Capaccio has written many different kinds of books for students. Some of them have been about history and some about science. He has even written his own science fiction, fantasy, and historical fiction stories. He also likes to perform international folktales as a professional storyteller for young audiences. He lives in Massachusetts with his wife Nancy and their golden retriever.